Contents

Applying for university can be a daunting exercise. Hopefully some of the tips and advice in this book will make that task much easier for you.

WHY BOTHER?

You're going to be at university for at least three years, so before we look at eveything else let's look at something very important.
What are the advantages of going to university?

You can become an expert in a subject you love
You can learn a huge amount about your favourite subject. You'll become an expert in your chosen subject. The chances are you'll also get to choose a number of specialist areas of study as your interests develop.

Graduates earn more
Graduates earn approximately 35% more than non-graduates, according to the Institute for Fiscal Studies (IFS). But don't forget that the 35% number is a headline – there are lots of factors which can make a difference. These include the course and university you choose and the career path you'd like to pursue.

Uni gives you time to gain work experience
Going to university means you'll be very highly qualified on graduation day, and some courses include a year in industry. Beware though, it doesn't guarantee you the technical and employability skills employers look for. Use the long summer holidays to gain experience and skills through internships, a summer job or work experience placement.

University can prepare you for a specific career path
Some jobs require a university degree. For example, if you want to be a doctor, nurse or a specific type of engineer, you'll need to go to university.

WHY BOTHER?

You'll become independent
Students prepare food and socialise together.
University is a good chance to learn the skills of
independent living. You may have to come out of your comfort zone
and you'll grow up quickly!

You'll probably ease in gently with a year living in halls of residence,
giving you the chance to learn basic life skills like cooking and doing
the laundry.

You will gain high-level transferable skills
A degree gives you skills that will stand you in good stead throughout
your career. Whatever subject you study, you'll learn to think
critically and analytically, question assumption, conduct thorough
and robust research, solve problems, and process large amounts of
information quickly.

It can broaden your mind
University is a chance to broaden the mind - many
students throw themselves into art, culture and politics.
One of the best things about uni is that it can alter your outlook on
the world. It's a chance to move to a new place, meet people from
different backgrounds, learn about fascinating ideas and experience
culture, art and politics.

ALTERNATIVES

It may be that you are not sure if university is for you or not. In that case, after college there are four other main options available to you

Take a gap year

This is when you take a year out before applying to university to have a think about what you want to do at university. You may have applied to enter university at a future date (called deferred entry) one year after your friends do and use this time to earn some money or go travelling.

Or it may be that you want to take the year out to really think about what you want to study and you use this time to research and get more experience, then apply to university.

What a gap year **IS NOT** is sitting on your backside for a year doing nothing. That is what is known as a huge waste of time. If you are taking a year out do something useful!

Find a job

This one is very straightforward, get your CV into shape and apply for jobs you like the sound of.

Find an Apprenticeship

The government is putting a lot of emphasis on these and the number of vacancies is growing. The difference between a job and an apprenticeship is that you will be gaining qualifications as well as getting paid as an apprentice.

Join the armed forces

This includes the Army, the Airforce and Royal Navy (The merchant navy is very different - they are sailors who work for private companies delivering goods across the oceans and do not get involved in conflicts)

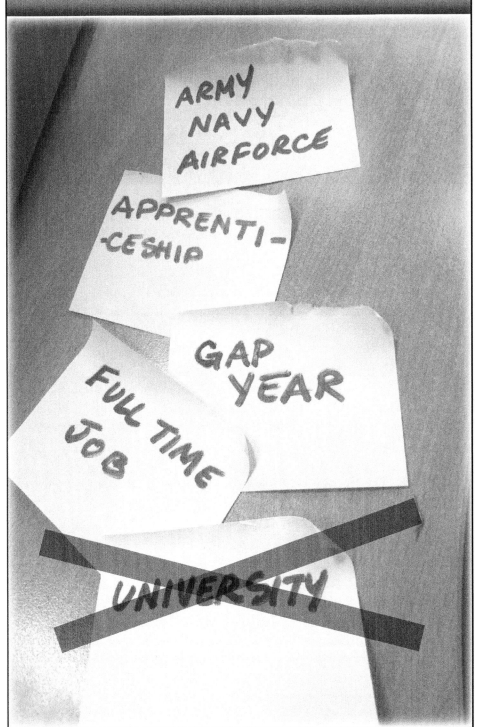

ELIGIBILITY

 **First things first, before anything else check that you are eligible to apply to university and that you can receive the appropriate funding.**

You can apply for full support if all the following apply:

You're a UK or Irish citizen or have 'settled status' (no restrictions on how long you can stay).

You normally live in England.

You've been living in the UK, the Channel Islands or the Isle of Man for 3 continuous years before the first day of your course, apart from temporary absences such as going on holiday.

You may be eligible for full support if you're a UK national (or family member of a UK national) who:

returned to the UK by 31 December 2020 after living in the EU, Switzerland, Norway, Iceland or Liechtenstein, has been living in the UK, the EU, Gibraltar, Switzerland, Norway, Iceland or Liechtenstein for the past 3 years.

You may also be eligible if your residency status is one of the following:

Refugee (including family members).

Humanitarian protection (including family members).

From the EU, Switzerland, Norway, Iceland or Liechtenstein (including family members) with settled or pre-settled status.

Child of a Swiss national and you and your parent have settled or pre-settled status under the EU settlement scheme.

Child of a Turkish worker who has permission to stay in the UK. You and your Turkish worker parent must have been living in the UK by 31 December 2020

A stateless person (including family members)

ELIGIBILITY

An unaccompanied child granted 'section 67 leave' under the dubs amendment.
A child who is under the protection of someone granted 'section 67 leave', who is also allowed to stay in the UK for the same period of time as the person responsible for them (known as 'leave in line').
Granted 'Calais leave' to remain.
A child of someone granted 'Calais leave' to remain, who is also allowed to stay in the UK for the same period of time as their parent (known as 'leave in line').
You've been given settled status ('indefinite leave to remain') because you've been the victim of domestic violence.
You've been granted indefinite leave to remain as a bereaved partner.

If you are eligible to apply, but not elligible for finance, it is worth investigating each universities' scholarship and bursaries on their websites.

TIME SCALES

So you know you are eligible, now is a good time to look at the timescales you are working with

N.B. *Dates not finalised by UCAS at time of publishing

April 2022	19 April 2022: UCAS' search tool will display 2023 courses.
May 2022	3rd may. You can register and start your application but cannot submit yet.
September 2022	7th Sept. Submission for applications opens.
Oct 2022	15 October DEADLINE entry at 18:00 (UK time) for any course at the universities of Oxford or Cambridge, or for courses in medicine, veterinary, and dentistry. You can add choices with a different deadline later, but don't forget, you can only have five choices in total.
Nov 2022 - Jan 2023	For all other courses: Research universities and courses and create a personal statement.
Jan 2023	25th January entry at 18:00 (UK time) DEADLINE for the majority of courses to guarantee they will be seen.
Feb 2023	22nd UCAS EXTRA opens.

TIMESCALES

Mar 2023	You can still apply up to June but there is no guarantee the univiersity will review your application
Apr 2023	
May 2023	By mid May (approx 19th) all applications before the Jan deadline will have had a decision sent to them.
June 2023	If you received a decision in May you need to reply by 9th June. Applications sent after 30th June are entered into clearing.
July 2023	4th July last date to apply to a course through Extra. 5th Clearing Opens.
Aug 2023	Results released

Even though UCAS deadline is in January - this is just the date that guarantees a university will look at your application. You can still apply after this date, but cannot guarantee that a university will look at it.

TIMESCALE OVERVIEW

1 **JANUARY, FEBRUARY, MARCH 2022**
Your college will have informed you of the
options available to you after you leave. You will
have been introduced to UCAs and various
online platforms to help you decide

APRIL - JUNE 2022
Begin to think about what you want to
do as a career. Ask why? What do you
need to get there? what personal
qualities will you need? **2**

SUMMER 2022
Take your time to go to open days and UCAS
fairs. Relax and rest as the hard work begins
3 after the summer

SEPTEMBER 2022
Register for UCAS and continue to research.
Work on your personal statement **4**

OCTOBER - DECEMBER 2022
Apply to your chosen universities
(Oct 15th deadline for Medicine, Dentistry
5 and Veterinary)
You may receive interview dates from December

6 **JAN, 2023**

UCAS cut off date (there is no guarantee universities will read your application after this date).
Arrange mock interviews with your careers team.

FEBRUARY, MARCH 2023

UCAS **Extra** opens. This gives you another opportunity to apply if you have declined all offers or been unsuccessful.
Start applying for finance in March.

7

8 **JUNE 2022**

Any application after this date automatically go into **Clearing**. Begin to plan what to take to University.

JULY 2023

Clearing opens.
Make sure you have your accommodation options sorted.

9

10 **AUGUST 2023**

A level/ Btec results are out and **Adjustment** opens

NUMBER OF COURSES

Guess how many courses are available at UK universities and colleges?
Go on, have a guess.

30,000!

Yep, that's 3 followed by 4 zeros

As you can see that's a pretty overwhelming number and you have to pick one of them.

Choosing a degree course is one of the most important decisions you'll make as a student. With 30,000+ courses and degrees offered by UK universities and colleges, this booklet will help you decide which one is just right for you.

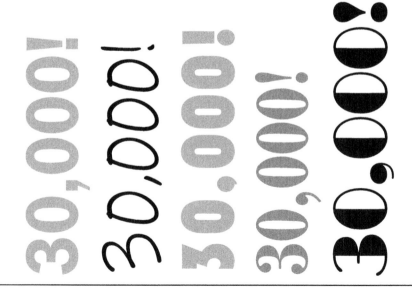

NUMBER OF UNIVERSITIES

131

There are 131 universities in the UK (plus many HE colleges and conservatoires)

That's a lot to chose from.
Do you want to live in a city?
On the coast?
In the countryside?
   Does the location matter to you at all?

Are you a home bird or want to get as far away as possible?
Do you want to go to
   Northern Ireland?
   Wales?
   Scotland?
      England?
      Did you know the most northerly university is the 'University of the Highlands & Islands' near Inverness

TYPES OF COURSES

Being an 'Undergraduate' simply means you are studying for a degree. A 'Postgraduate' means you have a degree and are continuing to study.

What types of undergraduate course are there?

After leaving school, most students going on to university or college study for an undergraduate degree. These are usually made up of modules (some compulsory and some optional) that add up to a full degree.

What is a BA and a BSc?

A BA is a bachelor of **Arts** (it simply means you have a degree in an arts based subject, not art itself)

a BSc is a bachelor of **Science** (it simply means you have a degree in a science based subject)

Sometimes the name of the course is included after the degree, for example BAEcon means you have a degree in Economics, BEng means you have a degree in Engineering

Honours Degree

A degree with honours, or an honours degree, is a standard three-year degree worth 360 credits, including a dissertation or special project in the final year of study. That's the 'honours' bit. As opposed to an ordinary BA or BSc, which is comprised of 300 credits and omits the dissertation or special project. On your degree certificate it will say BA(Hons) otherwise it will just say BA or MSc

What's a Masters?

This is a years worth of independent study that you can do after your degree. You usually need to propose a research topic that you will cover. You can apply to any university, you don't have to apply to the one you did your degree in. Masters are not available in all subjects and they can be competitive to get into.

TYPES OF COURSES

Bachelor degree courses

(The use of the name Bachelors for undergraduate degrees probably comes from the old French 'bachelor' meaning apprentice knight. This phrase referred to the lowest grade of knighthood.)

Bachelor degrees usually last either three or four years if studied full-time (although some courses are longer). You can concentrate on a single subject, combine two subjects in a single course (often called dual or joint honours courses), or choose several subjects (combined honours). Most courses have core modules which everyone studies, and many courses allow you to choose options or modules to make up a course that suits you.

For example,
Business **WITH** Law:
Is a course covering 75% for the first subject and 25% for the second.
Business **AND** Law:
Is a course covering 50% of each subject

Some bachelor degrees offer a sandwich year, involving an additional placement or year in industry, which forms part of the course. If you're an international student, you'll need to check if you're eligible to work in the UK, or that your visa allows you to do a placement course. Most international students on a tier 4 visa will be eligible for a year in industry or work placements as part of their course, but there may be some conditions. Check with the university or college before making this choice in your application.

TYPES OF COURSES

Foundation courses

Some degrees offer a foundation course. They are generally one year, full-time courses delivered at a university or college, and can be offered as a 'standalone' course, or as part of a degree. You'll still be treated as a full-time undergraduate student.

You may not have achieved the grades required or may not have studied appropriate subjects at A levels or BTEC.
Foundation courses are designed to develop the skills and subject-specific knowledge required to undertake a degree course. Most students who take a foundation year can stay at the same university if they pass the course.
If you think you won't hit the grades to do a degree or have not studied the right subjects at A level/BTEC, see if your university does a foundation course in the subject you want to study.

Diploma in Foundation Studies (art and design)

This one-year qualification – often shortened to 'Art Foundation' – is widely recognised as a primary route to gain entry to some of the most prestigious art and design degree courses. The learning is tailored to a student's specific area of art and design subject interests, so they can progress to study that area at degree level. For funding purposes, this course is classified as a further education course (FE), so student loans for tuition and living costs fees are not available, even if you take the course at a university or college. However, UK/EU students under the age of 19 on 31 August of the year of entry will NOT be charged a tuition fee. As a result, many students choose to take this course straight after school or college, in their hometown or city to avoid traveling and living costs.

Degree or graduate level apprenticeship

This is a type of higher level apprenticeship, which can lead to a bachelors degree as part of an apprenticeship. It is important to check the full details of a given job and apprenticeship with the employer and training provider. These courses are a good fit for students who want to gain work experience rather than studying full-time at university, but would like to achieve the same degree status.

HOW TO CHOOSE A COURSE

This is the biggie!
Of all the options available, how on earth do you pick a course that is right for you?

Things to consider:
What subjects are you good at?
What subjects do you like?
What are your hobbies?
What kind of books do you read?
What sort of TV or Nextflix shows etc. do you like to watch? Is it documentaries all about wildlife or about economics? Is it dramatic thrillers or love stories?
What are you passionate about?

Don't forget, you'll be at university for at least three years so make sure you study a subject that you'll enjoy. You may want to study something that you haven't covered in college e.g. Biochemical Engineering, Paramedic Science, Midwifery, International Studies. Make sure you research thoroughly, so you know exactly what you are letting yourself in for. And remember, each university will do their courses differently. A course in Psychology at Edinburgh university will contain different modules for the same named course at Sheffield. TAKE YOUR TIME! What subject would you like to immerse yourself in for 3 years?
Think about what kind of career you would like to go into.
Will your course help you progress towards that?
Take a look at
https://www.thecompleteuniversityguide.co.uk
to examine where each subject appears in league tables.

Use the
SCORING MATRIX
to help you decide

HOW TO CHOOSE A COURSE

You have

5 CHOICES

That means that you can pick 3 course at one university and another at a diffrent one and still another at a different one, or you can chose the same course at 5 different universities.

DON'T FORGET

You don't have to apply for them all at once, you can send your UCAs form off and log back in at another date and pick another choice until all five have been used up.

You don't necessarily have to have studied an A level in a particular subject to study it at degree level, for example you don't need A level law to do a law degree.

In terms of careers, you don't need to have a specific one in mind yet as a good degree will tell a potential employer that you are: smart, can work hard, can write documents, can organise yourself, can follow instructions, is motivated, hits deadlines...and all this before they even know what subject you studied.

Most course last for 3 Years, however be aware that some go on for much longer. Medical related courses are often much longer and law degrees can extend to many years (including training).

Some courses may have a year in industry or a year abroad which extends them to become a 4 year course.

Research, research, research.

If you are really stuck a good exercise is to get a sheet of paper and write 2 lists.

What I like e.g.- working with small kids, working outdoors

What I don't like e.g. Working with animals, working indoors all day

You can use this list to help you determine what you know you would **not like** to study.

COURSE INFO

Every course will have a unique identifying code and every university will have a unique code. It is useful to jot these down when you are researching as you will need them to fill in your UCAs form

Apply through UCAS

UCAS course code: H402

UCAS institution code: M20

Application codes

Course code: N400
Institution code: A40
Campus name: Main Site (Aberystwyth)
Campus code: -

Where do you find the codes?

On the universities' subject webpage there should be a code relating to that course. There may also be an institution code and a campus code (the campus code may not be relevant for many universities). If you cannot find them they will be listed on UCAS

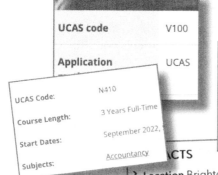

UCAS code: V100

Application: UCAS

UCAS Code: N410
Course Length: 3 Years Full-Time
Start Dates: September 2022,
Subjects: Accountancy

Key details

- A Levels **AAB**
  Other entry requirements
- UCAS code **C803**
- 4 years / Full-time

> **Location** Brighton: Falmer

> **UCAS code** L200

> **Full-time** 3 years

CAN YOU GET IN?

The very first thing you need to think about are the...

ENTRY REQUIREMENTS

Before you get heartbroken make sure you can match the entry grades required. Otherwise you may be completely wasting your time!
Each university course has its own entry requirements. These will specify the grades or UCAS tariff points and sometimes the subjects you'll need to get in.

You can apply for up to 5 universities. You can apply to study different courses at the same university.
Be aware, you may need to take extra exams if you want to study Law (LNAT exam) or Medicine (either a UCAT or BMAT exam depending upon which university you apply for).
You will also need minimum grades in Maths and English depending upon the university.

A* B M A CC A
D*D*P

MUST DO BETTER

TYPES OF UNIVERSITY

There are a few main things to consider when picking a university

OK, let's assume you are on target to get the grades required to study your subject, now you need to think about where you want to go.

Think about the University's **REPUTATION.**

Where does it come in the **LEAGUE TABLE?**

Is it a **RUSSELL GROUP** university? Is this important to you?

There are currently 24 universities belonging to the Russell Group:

RUSSELL GROUP

University of Birmingham
University of Bristol
University of Cambridge
Cardiff University
Durham University
University of Edinburgh
University of Exeter
University of Glasgow
Imperial College London
King's College London
University of Leeds
University of Liverpool
London School of
Economics & Political Science
University of Manchester
Newcastle University
University of Nottingham
University of Oxford
Queen Mary, University of London
Queen's University Belfast
University of Sheffield
University of Southampton
University College London
University of Warwick
University of York

These universities have a shared focus on research and a reputation for academic excellence. They tend to get huge government grants for their research and are often at the cutting edge of their subjects.

What are the league tables?

These are sets of tables created by different publishers e.g. The Times newspaper, the Guardian newspaper, the Complete Uni Guide, etc. They compare universities based on certain criteria, for example; student satisfaction rates, teaching ratios, research quality and graduate prospects.

These are not 100% accurate, because each league table has the universities in different positions within their league, depending upon what criteria they use and how they analyse it. However, they tend not to be too far off from each other.

What else to consider

Student satisfaction - connect with current students, most university websites now have a live chat area where you can speak to current students.

The physical environment

Go on open days and visit as many places as is practical and you will get a real feel for a place, not only the local area, but also the facilities and you'll get to experience the transport connections or how long the car journey is.

Clubs and societies

For example, if you are a really keen netball player is there a netball team you can become involved in?

Employability

Most universities now display the employability rates of their graduates, this is always worth looking at.

MEDICINE, VET, DENTISTRY

Medicine, Dentistry and Veterinary courses have a different cut off date to other courses. The cut off date is 15th October.

Applications to study medicine are also handled through UCAS. Applicants are able to apply for up to four medical courses. There are a very high number of applications to medicine each year and the process takes longer than most other courses. Medical schools are able to set their own entry requirements. Generally, the minimum entry requirements to medicine are three A level grades of A and above or equivalent qualifications. Usually two must be science based subjects (**chemistry is compulsory**) and some medical schools also require maths or physics at A level. Grades at GCSE or equivalent are usually considered as part of the application, but medical schools place varying emphasis on them.

As well as A levels you will need to do a separate exam in order to qualify for admission. The exam you take will depend upon the university you go to. There are two exams **BMAT** and **UCAT**. Opposite is a list of which universities require which exam.

• Your qualifications/predicted grades do not meet the course requirements.
• *Your UCAT/BMAT score was not high enough*
• *You didn't perform well at the interview*
• *Your personal statement was too weak**
*Not every medical school will give the same emphasis to statement.

In relation to dentistry and veterinary studies, these are even more competitive with few university degree places available
• 15 for veterinary science
• 14 for dentistry undergraduate
However, there may be options to apply to relevant foundation courses which can help with access to medical school

MEDICINE EXAMS

BMAT EXAM
Brighton & Sussex
Cambridge
Imperial
Lancaster
Leeds
Oxford
UCL

UCAT EXAM	
Aberdeen	Leicester
Anglia Ruskin	Lincoln
Aston Birmingham	Liverpool
Bristol	Manchester
Buckingham	UEA
Cardiff	Nottingham
Dundee	Plymouth
Edge Hill	Queen Mary
Edinburgh	Queens
Exeter	Sheffield
Glasgow	Southampton
Hull	St. Andrews
Keele	St. Georges
Kent & Medway	Warwick
King's College	York

UCAS TARIFF POINTS

A LEVEL	UCAS POINTS
A*	56
A	48
B	40
C	32
D	24
E	16

You can compare points
Many universities now accept both BTECS and A levels. The following graphs allows you to compare them. Some institutions may want a total number of points rather than specific subjects.

BTEC LEVEL 3 NATIONAL DIPLOMA	UCAS POINTS
D*D*	112
D*D	104
DD	96
DM	80
MM	64
MP	48
PP	32

UCAS tariff points	T Level overall grade	A level Equivalent
168	Distinction* (A* on the core and distinction in the occupational specialism)	AAA*
144	Distinction	AAA
120	Merit	BBB
96	Pass (C or above on the core)	CCC
72	Pass (D or E on the core)	DDD

WHAT ABOUT T- LEVELS?

T-Levels are a new qualification for 16–18 year-olds, introduced by the Government to give students more options to gain workplace skills. They are much more vocational than academic courses

Equivalent to 3 A levels
T Levels are an alternative to A levels, apprenticeships and other 16 to 19 courses. Equivalent to 3 A levels, a T-Level focuses on vocational skills and can help students into skilled employment, higher study or apprenticeships.

A 45-day industry placement
Each T Level includes an in-depth industry placement that lasts at least 45 days. Students get valuable experience in the workplace; employers get early sight of the new talent in their industry.

80% Classroom, 20% work
T Level students spend 80% of the course in the classroom, learning the skills that employers need. The other 20% is a meaningful industry placement, where they put these skills into action.

T = TRAINING

45 DAYS WORK PLACEMENTS

HOW TO USE UCAS

When applying to university you will apply online through the UCAS website. https://www.ucas.com/students

When you first register with UCAS use an email that is not your college one. You will be sent a code to that email that you then use to verify your account.

You will then see this message.

You will be asked which year are you applying for.

You will be asked which level are you applying for (this will be undergraduate).

You will be asked if you want further information on Apprenticeships and conservatoirs.

You will be asked to provide your postcode.

You will be asked for your preferences and whether you want to stay up to date with a variety of subjects.

You will need to include the college name and Buzzword.

HOW TO USE UCAS

Welcome to your Hub

You will then be presented to your hub

You can:
Highlight your favourites,
look at career options
review events coming up,
work out how many UCAS
points your grades are worth.

There are also areas relating to:
Writing personal statements,
timelines and deadlines,
what to study apprenticeships,
questions and answers and an area to keep all your notes.

Once you get into the UCAS hub go to 'START'.

You may get a security check. Follow instructions about entering an emailed code.

Click 'Undergraduate'.

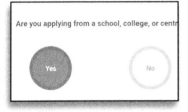

Click 'yes' you are applying from a college, even if you are not a current student.

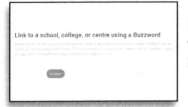

It will ask you to link to a college **Buzzword**.

HOW TO USE UCAS

Enter the Buzzword.

Make a note of it here

IMPORTANT!

Hit yes to confirm the buzzword.

You now need to select
'current student' or 'Oxbridge'
or Ex student if you have left college.

UCAS APPLICATION

You will then see a summary window

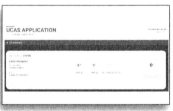

You will then see a window presenting
you with 'your choices'
and 'your profile'. These should be very
straight forward to fill in

If you are doing BTECs ensure you enter all of the modules you are
studying. Your teacher will be able to provide you with these.

REPLIES

Well done, you've sent off your application form. Now sit back and wait 'til you hear. Below is a breakdown of the replies you will receive

You met the Entry Reqs. Suitable statement. Good refs	Missed your Firm (favourite) offer	Declined all offers or had no offers	On results day not met requirements
⬇	⬇	⬇	⬇
Conditional offer (Possibly after an Interview)	Given **Conditional offer** by another university (Insurance)	Eligible for **UCAS EXTRA**	Eligible for **UCAS CLEARING**

Got better grades than expected

Eligible for UCAS **ADJUSTMENT**

What do 'firm' and 'insurance' mean?

Firm: this is your first choice – the place you most want to go to. If you accept a conditional offer and meet the conditions, you'll have a confirmed place there.

Insurance: this is the choice you'd want if you didn't meet the conditions of your firm choice. If this is a conditional offer, you'll need to meet the conditions, and then you'll have a confirmed place there.

COMMON UCAS QUESTIONS

UCAS Questions

I'm in Track but I don't have an option to reply to my offers.

This is usually because you haven't had a decision from all of your choices yet. However, if you're ready to reply and don't want to wait for the other choices to make a decision, you can choose to cancel them. To do this, click on 'view' for each outstanding choice and then you'll have the option to 'permanently withdraw from this choice.' Once you've done this, the 'reply to offers' button will be available in the 'Your choices' section of Track.

Can I reply to more than two offers?

You can accept a maximum of two choices – one firm and one insurance. You can only have an insurance choice if your firm choice is a conditional offer. If you accept an unconditional offer as your firm choice then the place is guaranteed, so you cannot have an insurance choice.

Do you have to reply to all your offers at the same time?

Yes, you have to reply to all your offers at the same time. But that doesn't mean you need to rush to make a decision as soon as you're in a position to reply. As long as you reply before the deadline date then your replies will be recorded. That said, it's not a good idea to wait until the last minute on your reply deadline day – so do give yourself enough time to reply carefully.

I've made a mistake with my replies. Can I change them?

You may change your replies once within fourteen days of initially making them. To do this, call UCAS with your Personal ID and an adviser will be able to help. Tel **03714680468**

When do I need to reply?

Once you've had decisions back from all of your choices, you'll be given a date in Track by which you need to reply.

WHAT IS UCAS EXTRA?

Extra gives you another shot if you have declined all or have not been successful with your applications. To be eligible, you must have used all five initial choices and not be holding any offers, or waiting for any decisions. If you're still waiting for decisions from some of your choices but you're certain you're not interested in these anymore and you don't want to wait for their decisions, you can cancel these outstanding choices. Then the **'Add an Extra choice'** option will become available. You should think carefully before doing this because you won't be able to reinstate these choices if you change your mind.

Make sure you reply to the offer by the date shown on your homepage, or your offer will be declined automatically.
If you decline the offer, or you don't get a decision within 21 days, you can add another choice. It might take universities and colleges longer than 21 days to reply, they have until midnight on 12 July to make their decisions, but it's up to you whether you want to wait or replace them with a different choice.
If you don't get the offer you want in Extra, don't worry, you can still use **Clearing** to add another choice.

I'm applying for a different subject, can I change my personal statement?
You can't change your personal statement, so if you're applying for a different course you may need to call the university and explain what you are doing and offer to send them a revised personal statement.

How many Extra choices can I make?
There's no limit to the number of times you can add an Extra choice to your application whilst Extra is running, but you can only ever have one being considered at any one time.

WHAT IS CLEARING?

Clearing is how universities and colleges fill any places they still have on their courses.

From 5 July – 18 October, you can apply for a course using Clearing if you're not already holding an offer from a university or college, and the course still has places.

You can use Clearing if:
you're applying after 30 June
you didn't receive any offers (or none you wanted to accept)
you didn't meet the conditions of your offers
you've paid the multiple choice application fee of £26.50
you've declined your firm place using the 'decline my place' button in your application

Clearing Plus

If you find yourself in Clearing this year, UCAS will personally match you to courses you may be interested in, using what they know about you from your application, and what universities and colleges are looking for in a student.

If you're unplaced or have started a new application, a button will appear in your application – '**My matches**'. This will take you to your top 50 course matches. You'll then be able to tell universities and colleges you're 'interested' in their courses. If they still have vacancies and you meet their entry requirements, they may call you.

Don't worry, if you want to apply for something different you can still find courses available in Clearing using the search tool.

STUDENT FINANCE

There are more myths about student finance than anything else. The bottom line is: borrow as much as you can from Student Finance, NOT the bank. It's not expensive to repay as you may think.

When you apply for a student loan you will see there are different repayment plans (The majority of you will be on Plan 2)
These are
Plan 1
Plan 2
Plan 4
Postgraduate Loan (Plan 3)
You cannot choose the repayment plan you're on. If you have more than one loan, they could be on different plans.

Plan 1
You're on Plan 1 if you're:
An English or Welsh student who started an undergraduate course anywhere in the **UK before 1 September 2012**
An Northern Irish student who started an undergraduate or post-graduate course anywhere in the UK after 1st September 1998
An EU student who started an undergraduate course in England or Wales after 1 September 1998, but before 1st September 2012
An EU student who started an undergraduate or postgraduate course in Northern Ireland on or after 1 September 1998

Plan 2
You're on Plan 2 if you're:

THIS WILL BE YOU

An English or Welsh student who started an undergraduate course anywhere in the UK **on or after 1 September 2012**
An EU student who started an undergraduate course in England or Wales on or after 1 September 2012.
Someone who took out an Advanced Learner Loan on or after 1st August 2013

STUDENT FINANCE

Plan 4
You're on Plan 4 if you're:
A Scottish student who started an undergraduate or postgraduate course anywhere in the UK on or after 1st September 1998
An EU student who started an undergraduate or postgraduate course in Scotland on or after 1st September 1998

PAY ATTENTION! *THIS MEANS YOU!*

The following pages will explain what you need to know about your loan and paying it back. Please go through the figures carefully so you really understand exactly what happens with your money.

STUDENT FINANCE

The first thing is to see whether you are eligible- see page 6 and 7

If you are, that's great.

There are a few things that will affect how much you will get:

- Your parent's or guardians household income
- Where in the country you want to study
- The Government's Student Finance rates

The loan that you receive is broken into two parts

```
            ┌──── STUDENT LOAN ────┐
            ↓                       ↓
```

TUITION FEE	MAINTENANCE LOAN
This goes straight to the university after you enrol. You never get your hands on it.	This covers your living expenses (travel, food, rent etc.) A third of this goes into your bank account, 3 times in the year

YOU HAVE TO RE APPLY EVERY YEAR

The current TUITION FEE per year is

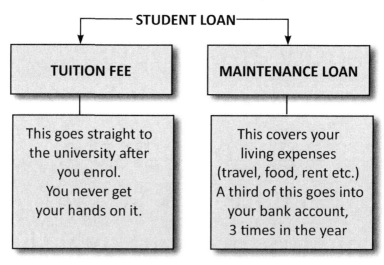

£9,250

STUDENT FINANCE

The current maximum MAINTENANCE LOAN
per year if you live AT HOME is

£8,171

The current maximum if you live outside
London, NOT AT HOME

£9,706

The current maximum if you live
IN LONDON, not at home

£12,667

Students with a disability can apply for additional support e.g. Non repayable finance, university bursaries and scholarships.
If you live at home you can still access this money.

STUDENT FINANCE

The amount you receive for your maintenance loan will be determined by your household income. In a nutshell, the more your parents earn the less loan you will get. (But the Tuition fee is payed in full)

The current threshold to receive the maximum is if your household income is less than

£25,000

A sliding scale is used to then work out what you can get. Please use the following website to calculate your loan

https://www.gov.uk/student-finance-calculator

Please Note: If you are studying one of the following courses you may be entitled to more:

Teacher training
Dental, Medical or Healthcare
Social work

One of the biggest worries students have is the thought of paying back all that money, before they begin to earn a wage, well...

DON'T PANIC

Mr. Mannering (ask your mum or dad)

The next few pages will explain how cheap and simple it all is.

STUDENT FINANCE

Here's how it works
You don't pay back anything, not a sausage until you have left university and once you're earning over a specified threshold. The current threshold is:

£25,000 per year

You'll pay 9% of anything you earn ABOVE that figure. Employers will deduct this automatically from your salary, like taxes, you won't notice it going and you do not need to do anything.

Your Wage £26,000 ↕ 9%

Threshold £25,000

Let's imagine you're at a stage in your career where you get paid over the threshold, you receive £26,000per year. This amount is £1000 above the threshold.

Therefore you will pay 9% per year on it

9% of £1000 = £90

In this instance you will be paying £90 PER YEAR back to Student Finance England

£90 Divided by 12 months = £7:50p per month

On a wage of £26,000 per year you will approximately receive £2,166 per month. After tax = £1,625 aproximately
So, £7.50 of that is a very small amount and should be easily affordable.

The money is taken directly from your pay by HMRC. You do not have to do anything

STUDENT FINANCE

Let's compare some diffent loan amounts

 Example 1

A student borrows £30,000 over the time of studying for their degree

They get a job that pays a salary of **£28,000** per year
£28,000 is **£3000** over the **threshold of £25,000**
They pay **9%** on that **£300** which is **£270** per year,
which is **£22.50** per month.
£270 per year x **40** years (after 40 years the loan is wiped off)
= **£10,800**
Over 40 years, £10,800 would be repaid (based on this salary)

Example 2

A student borrows £60,000 over the time of studying for their degree

They get a job that pays a salary of **£28,000** per year
£28,000 is **£3000** over the **threshold of £25,000**
They pay **9%** on that **£300** which is **£270** per year,
which is **£22.50** per month.
£270 per year x **40** years (after 40 years the loan is wiped off)
= **£10,800**
Over 40 years, £10,800 would be repaid (based on this salary)
So you see, they would pay back the same amount.
The loan amount is not the critical thing.

It is the amount of
pay you receive over the threshold

And if your annual wage falls below the threshold you stop paying.

You now pay back for 40 years

ACCOMMODATION

Do you want a Prince's palace or a pauper's place?

Universities make it easy for you in your first year as they provide student accommodation known as 'Halls of Residence'.

These are apartments set aside specifically for you. They are safe, comfortable and good value. These are usually furnished with a shared kitchen, toilet, bathroom, possibly a lounge area and en-suites. They're either catered, part-catered or self-catered, mixed or single-sexed, and can house any number up to 800 students. University halls of residence are great places to make friends and be part of the social scene and are great for support should you need it in those first few weeks and months away from home. However, they're can be loud and distracting (parties!) well into the beginning of the academic year.

Many universities will guarantee accommodation if you've firmly accepted their offer by a given date in the summer, though this isn't always the case if you gain your place through Clearing.

Most accommodation booking opens in March. You can book a room at your chosen university once you make them your FIRM CHOICE. They will send you an email about this

ACCOMMODATION

Below is a breakdown of the room types

En-suite

This would be like a Premier Inn room, you would have a bed, desk, wardrobe and your own bathroom. The seating and kitchen area will outside of the room in a communal area.

Shared

Can be very similar to en-suite however, the door opens on each side and you share your bathroom with one other person. More commonly, it is when you have your own room but share the bathroom and kitchen with up to 6 or 8 other students.

Self Catering

You can opt for catering or self catering for food. Most students have self catering whereby you cook for yourself. It will be useful to learn to cook now! If you choose catered, make sure it fits in with your lifestyle. For example you will have to pay for a breakfast will you be up to eat it? If you are vegan will there be a good choice?

Catered

Is when you have meals prepared for you and eat them in a canteen or dinning area. Breakfast, lunch and dinner is usually offered. Think whether you will be up in time for breakfast if you are paying for it in advance.
Make sure they cater for any needs you may have.

COMMON QUESTIONS

What if I change my mind about my course or university choices?

You can swap a choice for a different one within **14 days** of the date on your welcome email. You can only swap each choice once. However, you can't swap a choice after 30 June.

What if I cancel my application as I want to start again?

If you cancel your application you cannot reapply until the following year

What if I change my mind about my replies?

If you accepted your offers in the last 14 days, contact a UCAS adviser to make any changes to your replies.

If it's been more than 14 days since you replied to your offers, you'll need to speak to them about changing your replies, and then call UCAS to let them know what you want to do

Do I have to apply to all 5 choices at the same time?

Nope! You can apply to one or two then a while later go back into track and add more

Can I supply more than one Personal Statement?

This isn't possible. You can only upload one and you cannot amend it once its gone. If there are two courses you are applying for you need to try and make your statement cover both subjects. Unfortunately this isn't so easy sometimes. An option is to speak to the university about the fact your statement may not exactly be what they are looking for.

Can I reply to more than two offers?

You can accept a maximum of two choices – one firm and one insurance. You can only have an insurance choice if your firm choice is a conditional offer. If you accept an unconditional offer as your firm choice then the place is guaranteed, so you cannot have an insurance choice.

COMMON QUESTIONS

I'm in Track but I don't have an option to reply to my offers.

This is usually because you haven't had a decision from all of your choices yet. However, if you're ready to reply and don't want to wait for the other choices to make a decision, you can choose to cancel them. To do this, click on 'view' for each outstanding choice and then you'll have the option to 'permanently withdraw from this choice'. Once you've done this, the 'reply to offers' button will be available in the 'Your choices' section of Track.

Do you have to reply to all your offers at the same time?

Yes, you have to reply to all your offers at the same time. But that doesn't mean you need to rush to make a decision as soon as you're in a position to reply. As long as you reply before the deadline date then your replies will be recorded. That said, it's not a good idea to wait until the last minute on your reply deadline day – so do give yourself enough time to reply carefully.

I've made a mistake with my replies. Can I change them?

You may change your replies once within fourteen days of initially making them. To do this, call UCAS with your Personal ID and an adviser will be able to help. Tel **03714680468**

When do I need to reply?

Once you've had decisions back from all your choices, you'll be given a date in Track by which you need to reply.

Can I apply to an apprenticeship as well as a university place?

Yes you can. If you get offered both make sure you let the one you are turning down know about your decision.

What if I cancel my application as I want to start again completely?

If you cancel your application you cannot reapply until the following year.

COMMON QUESTIONS

Do universities actually read statements?

Yes and No. Some departments will look at them closely, others will not. There is no way of knowing. Our advice is to do the best one you possibly can. Imagine a university has a few students it cannot decide upon, it may use the statements as a decider.

Certain departments will definitely read statements e.g. Nursing, Midwifery, Social Work, Pharmacy, Paramedics

Do universities read statements if I'm applying for Art?

For art courses where they have asked for a portfolio of work, the majority of the decision whether to offer you a place will go on the quality of your work.

What if I feel really lonely and struggle to make friends?

Don't worry, you will not be alone in feeling this, it is very common. Contact the universities pastoral team. Also go along to any social events or join societies. If you are in shared accommodation maybe cook a meal for everyone on your floor.

There will be lots of very nervous and anxious students all in the same boat as you. Try and come out of your comfort zone a little and strike up a conversation with students on your course. A great way to do this is simply by asking questions

"Where have you come from?" " I'm so nervous about starting uni, how about you?" "What's A levels/BTECs did you do"?

Another great tip is to wedge your bedroom door open, so passers by can pop in to say hello. You can ebven put a sign up asking them in. This really breaks the ices

What if I change my mind about my replies?

If you accepted your offers in the last 14 days, contact a UCAS adviser to make any changes to your replies.

If it's been more than 14 days since you replied to your offers, you'll need to speak to them about changing your replies, and then call UCAS, to let them know what you want to do.

INTERVIEWS

What should I wear?

Always go smart (unless you've been specifically told not to).
Remember, you are out to impress remember. Looking smart shows
you have made and effort and are taking things seriously

What will they ask me?

They will want to know about your motivation for doing the course,
ask yourself why you want to study it, research the facilities at that
university. Think about what the challenges on the course will be
and why you would make a good student. If it is NHS related make
sure you know about the 6Cs of the NHS. Have a good knowledge
of your subject.
Nobody is trying to catch you out, they want to get the best out of
you. If it is online, prepare your space, have good lighting, look into
the camera and maybe have some notes around your screen so as
to prompt you. Practice, practice, practice

What if it's a group interview?

In a group interview they want to see how you interact with
other candidates. Don't be too outspoken or a wallflower either.
Try and involve others in the conversation if you can, so you can
demonstrate that you are a good team player.

Should I ask questions?

Yes, definitely if you get the opportunity. This shows that you know
about the course and what's involved.
Questions you can ask:
What do you think is the most challenging part of the course?
What careers do students tend to go on to?
How many people have applied?

SCORING MATRIX

How to use this matrix

Compare each component that is important to you and rank them from 1 to 10.

The ones with the highest score will be the ones most suited to you.

When you have done your research come back to here and insert your scores on the opposite page.

The first page of the matrix has a sample to show you how it works.

REMEMBER TO RESEARCH CAREFULLY AND MAKE SURE YOU VISIT YOUR TOP 3 CHOICES AT LEAST

MY TOP CHOICES

University Name	Subject	Total Scores
Flintshire	*Law (hons)*	96
University Name	Subject	
University Name	Subject	
University Name	Subject	
University Name	Subject	
University Name	Subject	
University Name	Subject	
University Name	Subject	
University Name	Subject	

University Name	Flintshire	Course	Law (hons)

Can I get the grades?   **Points**

Definitely = 10 pts	Probably = 7 pts	Possibly = 5 pts
Unlikely = 3 pts	No = 0 pts	

7

Are the modules for my subject right for me?

Definitely = 10 pts	Partially = 7 pts	Not really = 3 pts

7

Comments (change your score accordingly)

They do the modules on commercial law and land ownership in year 2 and a placement option. The lead lecturer also used to be a barrister

Extra points

4

Almost definitely, but not 10 points

Am I sure about this type of university?

Definitely = 10 pts	Partially = 7 pts	Not really = 3 pts

9

Do the hours suit my learning style?

Definitely = 10 pts	Partially = 7 pts	Not really = 3 pts

7

Is the location right for me?

Definitely = 10 pts	Partially = 7 pts	Not really = 3 pts

3

AFTER a visit how do you rate it out of 10

8

Comments after a visit

I thought a large city might be too noisy, but on the visit I saw how many quiet parks there were and loads of open spaces.

			Points
Can I cope with the transport options?			
Definitely = 10 pts	Probably = 7 pts	Possibly = 5 pts	
No = 0 pts	No = 0 pts		10
Are the facilities what I'm after?			
Definitely = 10 pts	Partially = 7 pts	Not really = 3 pts	3
Do the league tables back up my ideas?			
Definitely = 10 pts	Partially = 7 pts	Not really = 3 pts	10
Is the employability record good?			
Definitely = 10 pts	Partially= 7 pts	Not really = 3 pts	7
What do the students or ratings say?			
Brilliant = 10 pts	It's OK = 7 pts	Stay away = 0 pts	10

Comments after you speak to current or past students and do your research (change your score accordingly)

I thought there were no Kayaking clubs nearby but Marie (the student ambassador) told me that one exists south of the university

Extra points

5

Other comments that can affect your score, e.g. night life, accommodation, scholarships, societies.

I was worried about making friends and being lonely but Marie said everyone is in the same boat at first and each department has its own welcome party to make you feel at home.

Extra points

6

Total Score

96

University Name	Course

Can I get the grades? | Points

Definitely = 10 pts	Probably = 7 pts	Possibly = 5 pts
Unlikely = 3 pts	No = 0 pts	

[ ]

Are the modules for my subject right for me?

Definitely = 10 pts	Partially = 7 pts	Not really = 3 pts

[ ]

Comments (change your score accordingly)

Extra points

[ ]

Am I sure about this type of university?

Definitely = 10 pts	Partially = 7 pts	Not really = 3 pts

[ ]

Do the hours suit my learning style?

Definitely = 10 pts	Partially= 7 pts	Not really = 3 pts

[ ]

Is the location right for me?

Definitely = 10 pts	Partially = 7 pts	Not really = 3 pts

[ ]

AFTER a visit how do you rate it out of 10

[ ]

Comments after a visit

Can I cope with the transport options?			Points
Definitely = 10 pts	Probably = 7 pts	Possibly = 5 pts	
Unlikely = 3 pts	No = 0 pts		

Are the facilities what I'm after?		
Definitely = 10 pts	Partially = 7 pts	Not really = 3 pts

Do the league tables back up my ideas?		
Definitely = 10 pts	Partially = 7 pts	Not really = 3 pts

Is the employability record good?		
Definitely = 10 pts	Partially= 7 pts	Not really = 3 pts

What do the students or ratings say?		
Brilliant = 10 pts	It's OK = 7 pts	Stay away = 0 pts

Comments after you speak to current or past students
and do your research (change your score accordingly)

Extra points

Other comments that can affect your score, e.g. night life,
accommodation, scholarships, societies.

Extra points

Total
Score

University Name	Course

Can I get the grades?   Points

Definitely = 10 pts	Probably = 7 pts	Possibly = 5 pts
Unlikely = 3 pts	No = 0 pts	

Are the modules for my subject right for me?

Definitely = 10 pts	Partially = 7 pts	Not really = 3 pts

Comments (change your score accordingly)

Extra points

Am I sure about this type of university?

Definitely = 10 pts	Partially = 7 pts	Not really = 3 pts

Do the hours suit my learning style?

Definitely = 10 pts	Partially= 7 pts	Not really = 3 pts

Is the location right for me?

Definitely = 10 pts	Partially = 7 pts	Not really = 3 pts

AFTER a visit how do you rate it out of 10

Comments after a visit

Can I cope with the transport options?

Definitely = 10 pts	Probably = 7 pts	Possibly = 5 pts
Unlikely = 3 pts	No = 0 pts	

Points

[ ]

Are the facilities what I'm after?

Definitely = 10 pts	Partially = 7 pts	Not really = 3 pts

[ ]

Do the league tables back up my ideas?

Definitely = 10 pts	Partially = 7 pts	Not really = 3 pts

[ ]

Is the employability record good?

Definitely = 10 pts	Partially= 7 pts	Not really = 3 pts

[ ]

What do the students or ratings say?

Brilliant = 10 pts	It's OK = 7 pts	Stay away = 0 pts

[ ]

Comments after you speak to current or past students
and do your research (change your score accordingly)

Extra points

[ ]

Other comments that can affect your score, e.g. night life,
accommodation, scholarships, societies.

Extra points

[ ]

Total
Score

[ ]

University Name	Course

Can I get the grades?   Points

Definitely = 10 pts	Probably = 7 pts	Possibly = 5 pts
Unlikely = 3 pts	No = 0 pts	

[ ]

Are the modules for my subject right for me?

Definitely = 10 pts	Partially = 7 pts	Not really = 3 pts

[ ]

Comments (change your score accordingly)

Extra points

[ ]

Am I sure about this type of university?

Definitely = 10 pts	Partially = 7 pts	Not really = 3 pts

[ ]

Do the hours suit my learning style?

Definitely = 10 pts	Partially= 7 pts	Not really = 3 pts

[ ]

Is the location right for me?

Definitely = 10 pts	Partially = 7 pts	Not really = 3 pts

[ ]

AFTER a visit how do you rate it out of 10

[ ]

Comments after a visit

Can I cope with the transport options?

Definitely = 10 pts	Probably = 7 pts	Possibly = 5 pts
Unlikely = 3 pts	No = 0 pts	

Are the facilities what I'm after?

Definitely = 10 pts	Partially = 7 pts	Not really = 3 pts

Do the league tables back up my ideas?

Definitely = 10 pts	Partially = 7 pts	Not really = 3 pts

Is the employability record good?

Definitely = 10 pts	Partially= 7 pts	Not really = 3 pts

What do the students or ratings say?

Brilliant = 10 pts	It's OK = 7 pts	Stay away = 0 pts

Comments after you speak to current or past students
and do your research (change your score accordingly)

Extra points

Other comments that can affect your score, e.g. night life,
accommodation, scholarships, societies.

Extra points

Points

**Total
Score**

University Name	Course

Can I get the grades? | Points

Definitely = 10 pts	Probably = 7 pts	Possibly = 5 pts
Unlikely = 3 pts	No = 0 pts	

[ ]

Are the modules for my subject right for me?

Definitely = 10 pts	Partially = 7 pts	Not really = 3 pts

[ ]

Comments (change your score accordingly)

Extra points

[ ]

Am I sure about this type of university?

Definitely = 10 pts	Partially = 7 pts	Not really = 3 pts

[ ]

Do the hours suit my learning style?

Definitely = 10 pts	Partially= 7 pts	Not really = 3 pts

[ ]

Is the location right for me?

Definitely = 10 pts	Partially = 7 pts	Not really = 3 pts

[ ]

AFTER a visit how do you rate it out of 10

[ ]

Comments after a visit

Can I cope with the transport options?

Definitely = 10 pts	Probably = 7 pts	Possibly = 5 pts
Unlikely = 3 pts	No = 0 pts	

Points

[ ]

Are the facilities what I'm after?

Definitely = 10 pts	Partially = 7 pts	Not really = 3 pts

[ ]

Do the league tables back up my ideas?

Definitely = 10 pts	Partially = 7 pts	Not really = 3 pts

[ ]

Is the employability record good?

Definitely = 10 pts	Partially= 7 pts	Not really = 3 pts

[ ]

What do the students or ratings say?

Brilliant = 10 pts	It's OK = 7 pts	Stay away = 0 pts

[ ]

Comments after you speak to current or past students
and do your research (change your score accordingly)

Extra points

[ ]

Other comments that can affect your score, e.g. night life,
accommodation, scholarships, societies.

Extra points

[ ]

**Total
Score**

[ ]

University Name	Course

Can I get the grades? — Points

Definitely = 10 pts	Probably = 7 pts	Possibly = 5 pts
Unlikely = 3 pts	No = 0 pts	

Are the modules for my subject right for me?

Definitely = 10 pts	Partially = 7 pts	Not really = 3 pts

Comments (change your score accordingly)

Extra points

Am I sure about this type of university?

Definitely = 10 pts	Partially = 7 pts	Not really = 3 pts

Do the hours suit my learning style?

Definitely = 10 pts	Partially= 7 pts	Not really = 3 pts

Is the location right for me?

Definitely = 10 pts	Partially = 7 pts	Not really = 3 pts

AFTER a visit how do you rate it out of 10

Comments after a visit

Can I cope with the transport options? | Points

| Definitely = 10 pts | Probably = 7 pts | Possibly = 5 pts |
| Unlikely = 3 pts | No = 0 pts | |

Are the facilities what I'm after?

| Definitely = 10 pts | Partially = 7 pts | Not really = 3 pts |

Do the league tables back up my ideas?

| Definitely = 10 pts | Partially = 7 pts | Not really = 3 pts |

Is the employability record good?

| Definitely = 10 pts | Partially= 7 pts | Not really = 3 pts |

What do the students or ratings say?

| Brilliant = 10 pts | It's OK = 7 pts | Stay away = 0 pts |

Comments after you speak to current or past students
and do your research (change your score accordingly)

Extra points

Other comments that can affect your score, e.g. night life,
accommodation, scholarships, societies.

Extra points

Total
Score

University Name	Course

Can I get the grades?   Points

Definitely = 10 pts	Probably = 7 pts	Possibly = 5 pts
Unlikely = 3 pts	No = 0 pts	

[ ]

Are the modules for my subject right for me?

Definitely = 10 pts	Partially = 7 pts	Not really = 3 pts

[ ]

Comments (change your score accordingly)

Extra points

[ ]

Am I sure about this type of university?

Definitely = 10 pts	Partially = 7 pts	Not really = 3 pts

[ ]

Do the hours suit my learning style?

Definitely = 10 pts	Partially= 7 pts	Not really = 3 pts

[ ]

Is the location right for me?

Definitely = 10 pts	Partially = 7 pts	Not really = 3 pts

[ ]

AFTER a visit how do you rate it out of 10

[ ]

Comments after a visit

Can I cope with the transport options? | Points

Definitely = 10 pts	Probably = 7 pts	Possibly = 5 pts
Unlikely = 3 pts	No = 0 pts	

Are the facilities what I'm after?

Definitely = 10 pts	Partially = 7 pts	Not really = 3 pts

Do the league tables back up my ideas?

Definitely = 10 pts	Partially = 7 pts	Not really = 3 pts

Is the employability record good?

Definitely = 10 pts	Partially= 7 pts	Not really = 3 pts

What do the students or ratings say?

Brilliant = 10 pts	It's OK = 7 pts	Stay away = 0 pts

Comments after you speak to current or past students
and do your research (change your score accordingly)

Extra points

Other comments that can affect your score, e.g. night life,
accommodation, scholarships, societies.

Extra points

Total
Score

University Name	Course

Can I get the grades? | Points

Definitely = 10 pts	Probably = 7 pts	Possibly = 5 pts
Unlikely = 3 pts	No = 0 pts	

[ ]

Are the modules for my subject right for me?

Definitely = 10 pts	Partially = 7 pts	Not really = 3 pts

[ ]

Comments (change your score accordingly)

Extra points

[ ]

Am I sure about this type of university?

Definitely = 10 pts	Partially = 7 pts	Not really = 3 pts

[ ]

Do the hours suit my learning style?

Definitely = 10 pts	Partially= 7 pts	Not really = 3 pts

[ ]

Is the location right for me?

Definitely = 10 pts	Partially = 7 pts	Not really = 3 pts

[ ]

AFTER a visit how do you rate it out of 10

[ ]

Comments after a visit

Can I cope with the transport options?

Definitely = 10 pts	Probably = 7 pts	Possibly = 5 pts
Unlikely = 3 pts	No = 0 pts	

Points

[ ]

Are the facilities what I'm after?

Definitely = 10 pts	Partially = 7 pts	Not really = 3 pts

[ ]

Do the league tables back up my ideas?

Definitely = 10 pts	Partially = 7 pts	Not really = 3 pts

[ ]

Is the employability record good?

Definitely = 10 pts	Partially= 7 pts	Not really = 3 pts

[ ]

What do the students or ratings say?

Brilliant = 10 pts	It's OK = 7 pts	Stay away = 0 pts

[ ]

Comments after you speak to current or past students
and do your research (change your score accordingly)

Extra points

[ ]

Other comments that can affect your score, e.g. night life,
accommodation, scholarships, societies.

Extra points

[ ]

Total
Score

University Name	Course

Can I get the grades? | Points

Definitely = 10 pts	Probably = 7 pts	Possibly = 5 pts
Unlikely = 3 pts	No = 0 pts	

[ ]

Are the modules for my subject right for me?

Definitely = 10 pts	Partially = 7 pts	Not really = 3 pts

[ ]

Comments (change your score accordingly)

Extra points

[ ]

Am I sure about this type of university?

Definitely = 10 pts	Partially = 7 pts	Not really = 3 pts

[ ]

Do the hours suit my learning style?

Definitely = 10 pts	Partially= 7 pts	Not really = 3 pts

[ ]

Is the location right for me?

Definitely = 10 pts	Partially = 7 pts	Not really = 3 pts

[ ]

AFTER a visit how do you rate it out of 10

[ ]

Comments after a visit

Can I cope with the transport options? | Points

Definitely = 10 pts	Probably = 7 pts	Possibly = 5 pts
Unlikely = 3 pts	No = 0 pts	

Are the facilities what I'm after?

Definitely = 10 pts	Partially = 7 pts	Not really = 3 pts

Do the league tables back up my ideas?

Definitely = 10 pts	Partially = 7 pts	Not really = 3 pts

Is the employability record good?

Definitely = 10 pts	Partially= 7 pts	Not really = 3 pts

What do the students or ratings say?

Brilliant = 10 pts	It's OK = 7 pts	Stay away = 0 pts

Comments after you speak to current or past students
and do your research (change your score accordingly)

Extra points

Other comments that can affect your score, e.g. night life,
accommodation, scholarships, societies.

Extra points

Total
Score

University Name	Course

Can I get the grades?   **Points**

Definitely = 10 pts	Probably = 7 pts	Possibly = 5 pts
Unlikely = 3 pts	No = 0 pts	

Are the modules for my subject right for me?

Definitely = 10 pts	Partially = 7 pts	Not really = 3 pts

Comments (change your score accordingly)

Extra points

Am I sure about this type of university?

Definitely = 10 pts	Partially = 7 pts	Not really = 3 pts

Do the hours suit my learning style?

Definitely = 10 pts	Partially= 7 pts	Not really = 3 pts

Is the location right for me?

Definitely = 10 pts	Partially = 7 pts	Not really = 3 pts

AFTER a visit how do you rate it out of 10

Comments after a visit

Can I cope with the transport options?

Definitely = 10 pts	Probably = 7 pts	Possibly = 5 pts
Unlikely = 3 pts	No = 0 pts	

Are the facilities what I'm after?

Definitely = 10 pts	Partially = 7 pts	Not really = 3 pts

Do the league tables back up my ideas?

Definitely = 10 pts	Partially = 7 pts	Not really = 3 pts

Is the employability record good?

Definitely = 10 pts	Partially= 7 pts	Not really = 3 pts

What do the students or ratings say?

Brilliant = 10 pts	It's OK = 7 pts	Stay away = 0 pts

Points

Comments after you speak to current or past students and do your research (change your score accordingly)

Extra points

Other comments that can affect your score, e.g. night life, accommodation, scholarships, societies.

Extra points

Total Score

NOTES

NOTES

NOTES

NOTES

NOTES

NOTES

INDEX

ACKNOWLEDGEMENTS

Photo by Andrea Piacquadio from Pexels
Photo by Armin Rimoldi from Pexels
Photo by Keira Burton from Pexels
Photo by Tima Miroshnichenko from Pexels
Photo by William Fortunato from Pexels
Photo by Monstera from Pexels
Photo by Andrea Piacquadio from Pexels
Photo by Oladimeji Ajegbile from Pexels
Photo by RODNAE Productions from Pexels

Anthony John
is a post garduate qualified careers leader and has
helped 1000s of student on their
journey to university.
For more information or any queries
or suggestions, please email
Anthony John at
educationinprint@gmail.com

Printed in Great Britain
by Amazon

85818892R00047